Contents

Timeline

In this book you will find out what happened when the Romans invaded and settled in Britain. Use the timeline below to find how long ago the Romans came to this country.

▼ *Each section of the timeline represents 100 years. Find the date when the Romans invaded Britain. How many hundreds of years ago was this? Which other people came to Britain?*

Why move?

What reasons can you think of for people leaving the country where they are born, to live somewhere new? Here are two explanations to start you thinking.

We left our country because it was not safe to stay there.

Our family emigrated to Australia when my dad got a job here. We love the beach!

Britain is inhabited from about 8000 BC. In about 500 BC people called Celts move to Britain from around the River Rhine.

Romans invade Britain in AD 43, in the time of the Roman Emperor Claudius.

Roman rule of Britain ends in AD 410.

In the mid 5th century, Anglo-Saxons from northern Europe invade Britain and eventually settle there.

In 865 a Viking army sweeps through England and Vikings set up home there.

Vikings begin to attack Britain in 793.

Julius Caesar lands in Britain, 55-54 BC.

Britain is part of the Roman Empire for 350 years, until AD 410. The Roman army builds many roads in Britain.

300BC   200BC   100BC   0 AD   100   200   300   400   500   600   700   800

STEP-UP
HISTORY

Roman Invaders and Settlers

David Thorold and Simon West

Evans

First published in this edition in 2011
by Evans Brothers Limited
2A Portman Mansions
Chiltern Street
London W1U 6NR

Produced for Evans Brothers Limited by
White-Thomson Publishing Ltd,
2 St. Andrew's Place,
Lewes, East Sussex, BN7 1UP

Printed by New Era Printing Company Limited in
Chai Wan, Hong Kong, March 2011,
Job Number CAG1628.

Project manager: Ruth Nason

Designer: Helen Nelson, Jet the Dog

Consultant: Rosie-Turner Bisset, Reader in
Education and Director of Learning and
Teaching, Faculty of Education, University
of Middlesex

British Library Cataloguing in Publication Data

Thorold, David

Roman invaders and settlers - (Step-up history)

1. Romans - Great Britain - Juvenile literature

2. Great Britain - History - Roman period, 55
BC-449 AD - Juvenile literature

I. Title II. West, Simon

936.2'04

ISBN: 978 0 237 54378 5

Picture acknowledgements:
Bath Museum: page 22b; Bridgeman Art Library:
pages 5 (Musee de la Tapisserie, Bayeux, France,
with special authorisation of the City of Bayeux,
Giraudon), 6 (British Museum), 9b (Metropolitan
Museum of Art, New York), 10t (Louvre, Paris), 17t
(© National Museums of Scotland), 25b (©
Ashmolean Museum, University of Oxford), 27
(Museum of London); Camera Press: page 12;
Canterbury Archaeological Trust: page 16 and
cover (top right); Corbis: pages 1/8b (Charles and
Josette Lenars), 4/20t (Homer Sykes), 7t (Andy
Butler/Eye Ubiquitous), 9t (Archivo Iconografico, S.
A.), 18 and cover (Patrick Ward), 19t (Nik Wheeler),
25t (Jason Hawkes); Philip Crummy: page 14t;
Dorset County Museum: page 11; National Trust:
page 23b; Norwich Castle Museum: page 13t; St
Albans Museum: pages 19b, 21t, 21b, 23t, 26;
Topfoto: pages 7b, 13b, 14br and cover (top left),
15, 17b, 22t.

Maps by Helen Nelson.

Why the Romans came to Britain

The first Romans lived in Italy, around 2,750 years ago. Gradually their villages grew into a city-state called Rome. They fought and defeated other lands to build a great Roman Empire. You will see a map of it on page 8.

From the first century BC, Roman traders visited southeast and southwest Britain. Then, in 55-54 BC, a Roman general called Julius Caesar landed in Britain with a small army. He wanted to stop people in Britain from helping the tribes in Gaul (modern-day France), whom he was fighting. Caesar wrote a history which tells us that he defeated an army in Britain led by a chieftain called Cassivellaunus.

Caesar left Britain once the people had agreed not to help the Gauls. Nearly 100 years later, the Roman army came to conquer Britain and made it part of the Roman Empire.

▼ *This piece from Caesar's writings tells us that a tribe called the Belgae had invaded Britain in the past. What did the Belgae do after that?*

The interior portion of Britain is inhabited by those ... born in the island itself: the maritime portion by those who had passed over from the country of the Belgae for the purpose of plunder and making war ... and having waged war, continued there and began to cultivate the lands ... The climate is more temperate than in Gaul, the colds being less severe.

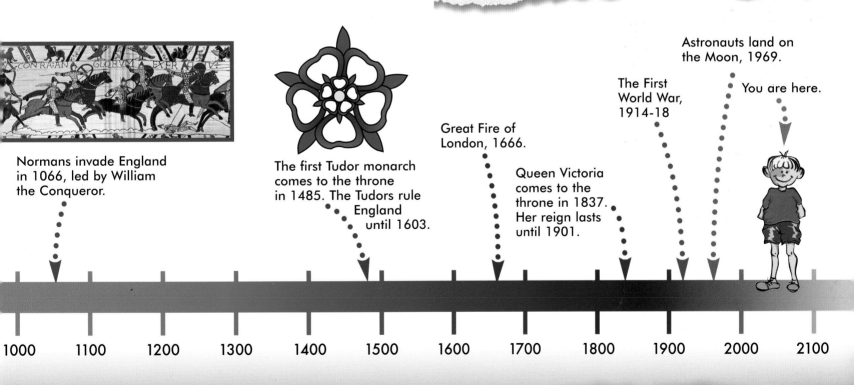

Normans invade England in 1066, led by William the Conqueror.

The first Tudor monarch comes to the throne in 1485. The Tudors rule England until 1603.

Great Fire of London, 1666.

Queen Victoria comes to the throne in 1837. Her reign lasts until 1901.

The First World War, 1914-18

Astronauts land on the Moon, 1969.

You are here.

1000   1100   1200   1300   1400   1500   1600   1700   1800   1900   2000   2100

5
••••

Find out about the Britons

Sources of information

Roman traders bought goods from Britain which included woollen cloaks, hunting dogs, gold, tin, corn and slaves. What information about Britain would these goods give to other Romans?

Julius Caesar's writings also told the Romans about Britain and its people, the Britons. From Caesar's writings here and on page 5, what opinion do you think Caesar had of the Britons? Did he admire them?

▶ *Caesar's writings help us to find out about the Britons at the time he was in Britain in 55-54 BC. What does Caesar say the Britons used for money?*

▶ *Archaeologists found this gold coin, marked with the name of Tincommius, a chieftain who ruled part of southern Britain in the first century BC. Does this archaeological evidence contradict what Caesar says?*

The most civilised ... are they who inhabit Kent, which is entirely a maritime district ... Most of the inland inhabitants do not sow corn, but live on milk and flesh, and are clad with skins. All the Britons dye themselves with woad, which occasions a bluish color, and thereby have a more terrible appearance in fight. They wear their hair long, and have every part of their body shaved except their head and upper lip.

The number of the people is countless, and their buildings exceedingly numerous, for the most part very like those of the Gauls: the number of cattle is great. They use either brass or iron rings, determined at a certain weight, as their money. Tin is produced in the midland regions; in the maritime, iron; but the quantity of it is small: they employ brass, which is imported. As in Gaul, there is timber of every description, except beech and fir. They do not regard it lawful to eat the hare, and the cock, and the goose; however, they breed them for amusement and pleasure.

What information given by Julius Caesar, and by British goods, might make the Romans want to add Britain to their Empire?

Most Britons lived in roundhouses, sometimes in small villages. Using evidence from excavations, archaeologists have built reconstructions of the houses, which help us to imagine what they were like.

Who were the Britons?

The Britons were made up of different tribes, each ruled by its own chieftain. Chieftains came from the warrior class, the top level of society, who owned large farms and areas of land. Priests, known as druids, were equally important.

Most other people were farmers. Some were slaves, captured in battle or on raids. A few craftsmen specialised in making pots and metal tools.

Building a roundhouse

Visit http://www.bbc.co.uk/history/interactive/animations/ironage_roundhouse/index_embed.shtml and see the skill that was needed to build a roundhouse.

Clothing

From studying Roman writings, historians think that the Britons wore colourful patterned tunics and trousers, with long woollen cloaks.

Religion

The Britons worshipped many different gods and goddesses across the country, and sometimes built shrines and temples to them. It seems that human heads were important to the Britons. Some shrines were decorated with model heads, or possibly real ones.

Some houses were grouped in a hill fort, a defended area on a hilltop, surrounded by ditches and ramparts. These are the remains of a hill fort known as Maiden Castle.

How were the Romans different?

The Roman Empire

This map shows the lands that were part of the Roman Empire in the early 1st century AD, and the lands that were conquered in the next 100 years. Each part of the Empire was known as a province. Every province was run by a governor, appointed by the Emperor. The provinces all had to pay taxes and provide troops for the Roman army. So, as the Empire expanded, Rome became richer and more powerful.

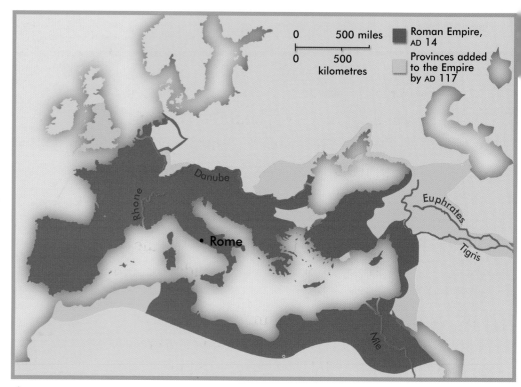

0	500 miles	Roman Empire, AD 14
0	500 kilometres	Provinces added to the Empire by AD 117

Compare this map of the Roman Empire with a modern atlas map. Which modern countries were part of the Empire?

The Roman army was made up of units called legions, of 3,000 to 5,000 men. These men are dressed to show what foot soldiers, called legionaries, looked like.

The Roman army

The Roman army was different from most armies in the ancient world. Soldiers in the Roman army served full-time for 25 years and were highly trained. When a soldier retired, he was made a Roman citizen and given a plot of land. Often this had been taken from defeated enemies. Most ancient armies were formed from local people who went back to work on their farms when a battle was over.

Citizens, non-citizens and slaves

Roman citizens had a special status in society. They had the right to vote and did not pay taxes. At first, only men from Rome could be Roman citizens. Men in other parts of the Empire could earn citizenship, usually by serving in the Roman army. Roman women and most other people in the provinces were non-citizens and had limited rights. By the third century AD, the rules were relaxed and more people were made citizens.

Many Romans kept slaves, some of whom were enemy soldiers captured in battle. Slaves were often given the worst jobs, such as mining, working on the land or fighting as gladiators, but some well-educated slaves became scribes or clerks. After long service, some slaves were freed, as a gift from their master.

▲ This carving of a banquet, from a Roman tomb, gives us information about clothing and hairstyles.

▶ This wall painting from an ancient Roman house at Pompeii dates from the first century BC. What does it tell you about Roman buildings?

List the differences

Make a table, showing all the differences you can find between the Romans and the Britons (pages 6-7). Were they similar in any ways?

9

The Romans invade Britain

Reasons to attack

The Emperor Claudius had several reasons for attacking Britain in AD 43:

- Roman traders had shown that Britain was wealthy.
- He was not popular in Rome and thought that conquering a new land would help to change this.
- Some people claimed that Britons were attacking and raiding Roman Gaul.

◀ *Claudius was the fourth Roman Emperor, who ruled from AD 41 to 54. He hoped that a military victory would make him popular with the Romans.*

The Britons react: some for ...

Some chieftains in Britain had traded with Romans and visited Roman towns. Once the Romans invaded, it looked probable that Britain would become a province of the Roman Empire. The chieftains saw advantages in this. They hoped they could stay in power in the new province.

... some against

Other chieftains fought the Romans. One tribe, the Catuvellauni, had recently invaded the lands of another tribe, the Trinovantes, who supported Rome. The leaders of the Catuvellauni, Caratacus and Togidumnus, formed an army to fight the Romans.

▼ *The Romans conquered Britain over the course of nearly 40 years. Which tribe or tribes were in the area where you live?*

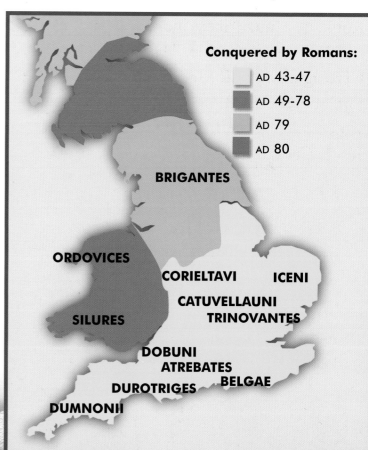

Conquered by Romans:

AD 43-47
AD 49-78
AD 79
AD 80

BRIGANTES

ORDOVICES

CORIELTAVI   ICENI

CATUVELLAUNI

SILURES   TRINOVANTES

DOBUNI

ATREBATES

BELGAE

DUROTRIGES

DUMNONII

The Romans attacked the hill fort at Maiden Castle in AD 44. Archaeologists have uncovered skeletons of people killed there. One had a Roman *ballista bolt* in the spine.

It doesn't look as if the rest of the Catuvellauni joined in. If they had, their lands would have been damaged by the Romans. Archaeologists have found that the lands were left unharmed.

Caratacus and Togidumnus formed their army from people who were willing to fight the Romans. Some tribes, including the Iceni, did not support either side. The northern tribes were against the Romans, but may not have joined in the fight, believing that Claudius would soon leave Britain, in the same way as Julius Caesar had done.

For or against?

Would you have welcomed the Romans or fought against them? What arguments would you use to persuade someone to agree with you?

Roman victory

Accounts by Roman writers say that the British were defeated. Togidumnus was killed and Caratacus fled. After twelve weeks of battle, Claudius celebrated victory at Camulodunum (modern Colchester) with a parade including elephants. What impression do you think these animals made on local people?

After this the Roman army advanced into the midlands and southern England. Caratacus led the fight against them. Some tribes retreated to their hill forts, but the Romans destroyed these easily. It took the Romans about four years to make sure that the south of Britain was secure. Look at the map on page 10 to find which part of Britain they attacked next.

Rewards

Tribes that welcomed the Roman invasion were rewarded. The Catuvellaunian town of Verulamium (modern St Albans) was given a special status as a municipium. Its inhabitants were made Roman citizens. One British leader had a palace built for him at Fishbourne.

The start of a revolt

Prasutagus, king of the Iceni

The Iceni stayed neutral when the Romans invaded Britain, and the Romans rewarded them for this by allowing the Iceni king, Prasutagus, to stay in full control of the tribe and its land. The Romans intended that, once Prasutagus had died, his kingdom would become part of the Empire. But Prasutagus hoped that the tribe could keep its special status and so he named his daughters and the Emperor Nero as his joint heirs.

Prasutagus died in AD 60 and the Romans started to treat the Iceni just as other British tribes. They took people's land, saying that it was payment for debts, and gave it to Romans.

Boudica becomes a leader

When Boudica, the wife of Prasutagus, and her daughters complained, the Romans replied by beating them violently. This made Boudica even more angry and she rallied the Iceni to revolt against the Romans.

◄ This statue of Boudica and her daughters in their chariot was sculpted at the very end of Victorian times. What impression of Boudica does it convey?

People from the Trinovantes tribe joined Boudica's army. Land in their area, at Camulodunum, had also been taken from local people and given to retired Roman soldiers. This was normal Roman practice, but the soldiers took much more land than they were allowed. The Trinovantes, like the Iceni, believed that they were favoured allies of Rome and they were unhappy with such harsh treatment.

What did Boudica look like?

No picture of Boudica has survived from the time when she was alive, although we have this description of her from a Roman historian, Cassius Dio, who lived in the 2nd century.

▲ The Norwich Castle Museum has a special section about Boudica and the Iceni people.

▼ A torc was a piece of jewellery worn around the neck. This one was made from more than a kilogram of gold mixed with silver.

Boudica was tall, terrible to look on and gifted with a powerful voice. A flood of bright red hair ran down to her knees, she wore a golden torc made up of ornate pieces, a multi-coloured robe and over it a thick cloak held together by a brooch. She took up a long spear to cause dread in all who set eyes on her.

Wanted: Boudica

Use Cassius Dio's description of Boudica to make a 'Wanted' poster for her. Compare posters drawn by your friends. What is similar and what is different in your pictures?

Boudica's revolt

Follow the route that Boudica's army took, on the map at the bottom of this page.

Camulodunum

First the army marched south to attack Camulodunum, a town of Roman citizens. There were few Roman soldiers there to defend the town. Most were with the Roman governor, Suetonius Paullinus, fighting the tribes in Wales. Camulodunum was destroyed and everyone killed.

▼ *Archaeologists think that Boudica's army followed this route in AD 60-61. More and more people joined in along the way.*

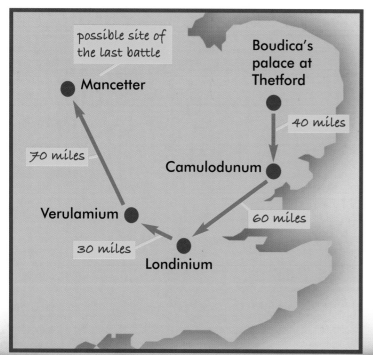

possible site of the last battle

Mancetter

Boudica's palace at Thetford

40 miles

70 miles

Camulodunum

Verulamium

60 miles

30 miles

Londinium

▲ *Archaeologists have found the remains of buildings burned down by Boudica's army at Camulodunum.*

▶ *This head from a life-size statue of Emperor Claudius was found in a river in Suffolk. It is thought that Boudica's army may have broken the statue and thrown the head into the water.*

The legion closest to Camulodunum had tried to march to the town to help, but Boudica's forces defeated them too. Paullinus ordered his army to return from Wales to crush Boudica's revolt.

Londinium

Boudica's next target was Londinium (London), another new Roman town. It was a port and could be used to bring in more Roman soldiers. It was also full of money and valuables.

Paullinus and his cavalry reached London before Boudica's army. However, they were too few to defend the city and so Paullinus withdrew and rejoined the rest of his army. Boudica's army destroyed Londinium and moved on to Verulamium.

▲ *These skulls found in London may be those of people massacred by Boudica's army.*

Verulamium

The inhabitants of Verulamium were Britons from the Catuvellauni tribe who supported the Romans. They heard that Boudica was on her way and probably had time to escape before the town was destroyed.

The final battle

By now the Roman army was back from Wales and ready to fight. Paullinus had around 10,000 men. Boudica's army was much bigger – more than 100,000. They were so confident of victory that they brought their families to watch the battle, from wagons behind the troops. Yet the Britons were defeated and, when they tried to flee, they were trapped by the wagons behind them.

A Roman historian, Tacitus, wrote that 80,000 Britons and only 400 Romans were killed.

Headlines

Try writing newspaper headlines for reports of what happened at each place that Boudica's army attacked.

The Romans had the advantage of being at the top of a slope, protected on one side by forest. The Britons were on the plain below. The site of this last battle has never been found, but it may have taken place near Mancetter in Warwickshire.

Afterwards, Boudica either committed suicide or died of natural causes. Paullinus became a famous general because of his heroic victory.

The effects of the revolt

Punishing Boudica's followers

After defeating Boudica and her followers, the Roman army attacked the lands of the Iceni and Trinovantes. Farms and villages were destroyed and anyone suspected of being involved in the revolt was killed or sold as a slave. Land and valuables were given to Romans or passed into the control of Emperor Nero, who ruled from AD 54 to 68.

Preventing more revolts

The Romans were worried that other tribes in the south might attack them. They stopped fighting in Wales and northern England and spent the next ten years strengthening their control in the south.

Points of view

Think what
(a) a Briton and
(b) a Roman soldier would say to explain how their life changed after the revolt.

After Boudica and h army were defeated things changed ...

The new Roman governor took more notice of the Britons' concerns. Important Britons were made Roman citizens and councillors, with responsibility for enforcing the law and collecting taxes. Warriors from the British tribes were encouraged to go back to farming rather than fighting.

◀ Some Britons had Roman-style villas built for them. This is a reconstruction drawing of a villa, based on archaeological evidence found at Maidstone, Kent.

Continuing the invasion

By AD 71 the Roman army advanced again into Wales and northwest England. More battles took place with the British tribes in these regions. In AD 82 or 83 the Ninth Legion was almost destroyed in battle against tribes in Scotland. Very little information about the defeat was recorded by Roman writers. Why might this have been? Despite such problems, the Romans slowly gained control of Britain.

◀ This carving in Scotland from about AD 142 shows a Roman cavalryman. Fighting against the British tribes continued for many years.

▼ The Romans built forts to protect their soldiers. Each had a wall of turf or stone, with a ditch outside to make it difficult for attackers to reach. Forts had a regular layout with an officers' headquarters, barrack blocks for the troops, and granaries to store food. This is Housesteads fort on Hadrian's Wall.

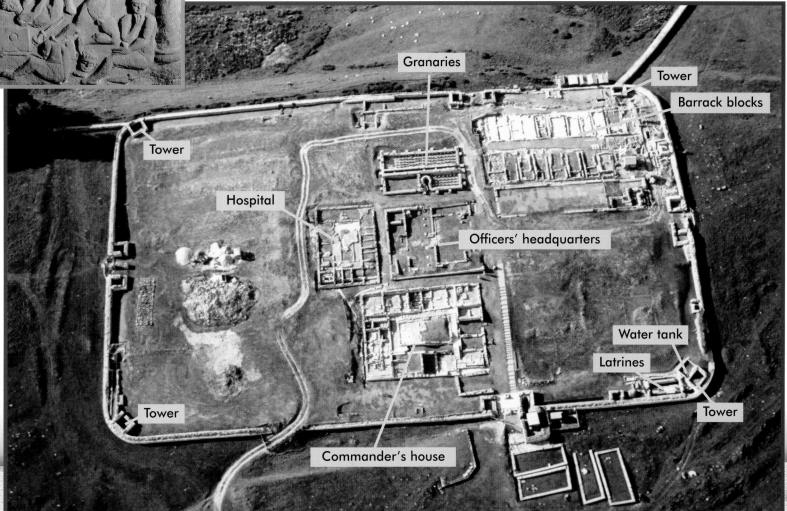

Granaries

Tower

Barrack blocks

Tower

Hospital

Officers' headquarters

Water tank

Latrines

Tower

Tower

Commander's house

The province of Britannia

The Romans fought in Scotland but eventually decided not to occupy this part of Britain. In AD 122 Emperor Hadrian, the 14th Roman Emperor, ordered a wall to be built, marking the limits of the Roman Empire. England and Wales were under Roman control and were known as the province of Britannia.

▼ *Hadrian's Wall ran from the River Solway to the River Tyne. See if you can find it on an atlas map of Britain.*

Civilising the province

The Romans allowed local customs to continue in new provinces of the Empire, as long as the people obeyed Roman rule and paid their taxes. However, Britannia seemed backward to them and they set about civilising it by developing towns and introducing Roman laws and customs. They hoped that the Britons would adopt a Roman lifestyle, after seeing its advantages.

Roman towns

The Romans built a town in each tribe's territory, with wooden, stone and brick buildings that were bigger than anything built in Britain before. Some had mosaics laid into the floors. Some houses also had painted walls and ceilings and even central heating. Hot air from a fire circulated through hollow bricks in the walls and along spaces dug below floors.

You can see where hot air circulated below the floor of this mosaic.

Mosaics were made from small, coloured stone squares called tesserae.

Towns had public buildings where business was carried out and people could meet. Each town had a forum, a large open space for a market. There were also temples and a basilica, a building for council business. Some towns had theatres for plays and religious activities, while others had amphitheatres.

The bath house

The most popular Roman entertainment was the bath house, a building with heated rooms and pools of hot, warm and cold water for bathing. To the Romans, bath houses were a place to meet, and the Britons quickly adopted their use. Visit http://www.romanbaths.co.uk/ and click on 'Children's pages' to tour a Roman bath house.

Your town

Think about buildings in your town which have a particular purpose. Which are similar to buildings in Roman Britain?

How the Romans changed Britain

After the invasion, the Romans controlled Britain for about 350 years. During that time, they made many changes to the British way of life.

Wider roads and more trade

Britons lived near their farms and traded with people close by for goods that they could not produce themselves. Their settlements were linked by trackways across the countryside.

The Romans built wide roads to allow their troops to move quickly around the province. The new roads linked villas, towns and ports across Britannia. One important result was that goods became more widely available to more people.

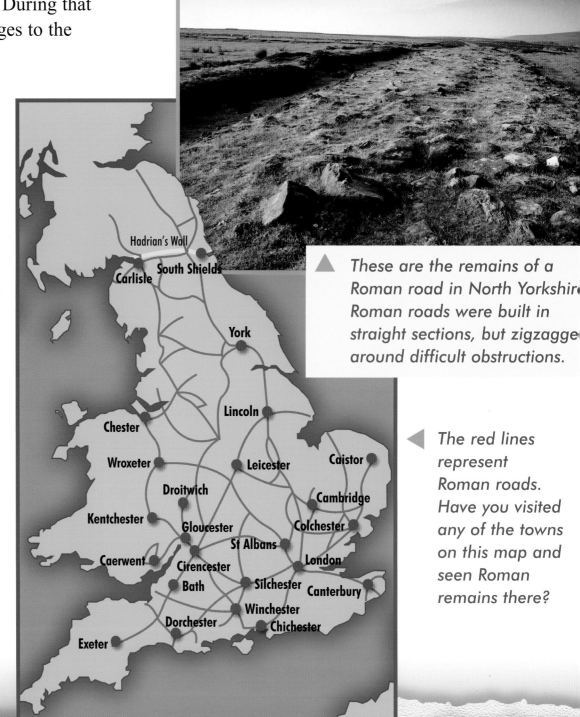

▲ These are the remains of a Roman road in North Yorkshire. Roman roads were built in straight sections, but zigzagged around difficult obstructions.

◄ The red lines represent Roman roads. Have you visited any of the towns on this map and seen Roman remains there?

Map labels: Hadrian's Wall, South Shields, Carlisle, York, Lincoln, Chester, Wroxeter, Leicester, Caistor, Droitwich, Cambridge, Kentchester, Gloucester, Colchester, St Albans, Caerwent, Cirencester, London, Bath, Silchester, Canterbury, Winchester, Dorchester, Chichester, Exeter

Buying and selling

Some British tribes made coins, although these were not widely used. Most Britons bartered their produce or services for anything they needed. By contrast, across the Empire, the Romans used coins of gold, silver or bronze to pay for goods and services.

Trade was more complicated in Roman society. As well as farmers, there were many people in other professions including potters, metalworkers, carpenters, plumbers, bakers, stonemasons and teachers. Roman craftsmen could not rely on finding a buyer willing to barter every time they needed food or clothes. Coins were a form of payment that everyone could accept. Money could also be saved to buy more or better-quality possessions.

With the spread of roads and the use of coins, trade and industry developed quickly in Britannia. Farmers could save the money they made from selling their crops until it was needed. Craftsmen could sell their wares across the country.

Some British products became so popular that they were sold across the country. This pot made in Peterborough was found at St Albans.

Trade also developed with other parts of the Empire. New foods such as cabbages, carrots, parsnips, turnips, plums and walnuts were imported into Britain, along with wine, olive oil and fish sauce. British grain, wool and hunting dogs were exported.

These are amphorae, which the Romans used for transporting wine and other liquids. Roman wine was popular with wealthy Britons, but most people drank ale.

Imports today

Which foods can you find in your kitchen today which have been imported? Make a list showing the countries they have come from. Find them on a globe.

How did Britain stay the same?

Rich and poor

Generally, it was the richer Britons who adopted the Roman lifestyle. The poor had little contact with it. Most Britons continued to speak their local language, for example, Brythonic. Only Britons involved with local government, law or trade needed to use Latin, the official Roman language. Also, any Briton wanting to improve his position in society needed to speak Latin.

Only the rich could afford a grand Roman villa like the one on page 16. Most Britons continued to live in roundhouses and to farm as they had always done. Archaeologists excavating small farms from this time have found very few Roman objects. Only about 10 per cent of the population lived in towns, where the Roman influence on life was stronger.

This Latin inscription is from the tombstone of Marcus Cocceius Nonnus, aged 6. Here are the Roman numerals for '6'. 'Hic situs est' is Latin for 'He lies here'.

Religion

The Britons worshipped many different gods, each responsible for a particular place or aspect of life such as the harvest, music, or success. This was similar to the Romans' religion, and so the Romans simply combined matching gods together. For example, Mars and Toutatis, the Roman and British gods of war, became Mars-Toutatis.

Sulis-Minerva was a combination of the British and Roman goddesses of wisdom.

Clothing

Clothing styles changed little for most working people. Amongst wealthy Britons, Roman tunics, short hair and a clean-shaven face were fashionable for men, although beards were popular in the second century. Wealthy women adopted the latest Roman hairstyles.

Togas, which were worn as a symbol of Roman citizenship, were not common in Britain. They were complicated to put on and cold and uncomfortable to wear, so they were kept for special occasions only.

▶ *This bone hairpin shows the Roman hairstyle that was fashionable in about AD 100. The necklaces are made from glass, jet, shale and gold foil.*

◀ *This part of a mosaic at Chedworth Roman villa in Gloucestershire represents 'Winter'. It shows a Briton in a hooded cloak, a traditional British garment, which the Romans called the 'birrus Britannicus'. The cloaks were one of Britain's main exports.*

Design a mosaic

Design and make a model of a mosaic floor, using little squares of coloured paper. Choose a subject to do with Roman Britain, and make a pattern around the edge.

The end of Roman Britain

From the map of the Roman Empire on page 8 you can see that Britannia was one of the most distant provinces from Rome. It provided the Empire with grain and wealth through the taxes that people had to pay. On the other hand, it was expensive to keep in good order, with four legions based there.

Two Empires

By AD 286 the Roman Empire had become too big for one Emperor to control. It was split into an Eastern and a Western Empire, each ruled by a different Emperor. Sometimes this worked well, usually when the two Emperors were brothers, or a father and son. However, the two Emperors often plotted against each other. Each hoped to replace the other with someone under their control. Sometimes this led to civil war, with Roman armies fighting each other. Soon army generals realised that they could use the troops they commanded to make a bid to become Emperor themselves.

Create a coin

Draw yourself as a Roman Emperor on a coin. How can you write your name so it sounds Latinised? Give yourself an important-sounding title, such as 'Scorer of Goals' or 'Maker of Music'.

◄ One side of this gold coin made in London at the end of the fourth century shows the Eastern and Western Roman Emperors holding a globe of the world.

◄ The other side shows Magnus Maximus, an army general in Roman Britain. In AD 383 he withdrew troops from Britain as he tried to win power in Rome. He fought his way to Italy, killing the Emperor of the West. Eventually he was defeated and put to death by the Emperor of the East.

Barbarians

The Romans called anyone from outside the Empire a 'Barbarian'. Barbarians had been raiding or trying to settle in the provinces since the Empire was formed. By the fourth century, so many Barbarians were in the Empire that more troops were needed to control or fight them.

The legions leave

By AD 400 most Roman soldiers based in Britain had been removed. Some had left with generals who tried to become Emperor. Others were moved to fight Barbarian forces who were attacking other parts of the Empire.

Eventually there were no legions left in Britain. In AD 410 the population asked for replacements. Emperor Honorius replied that no troops were available and the people would have to defend themselves.

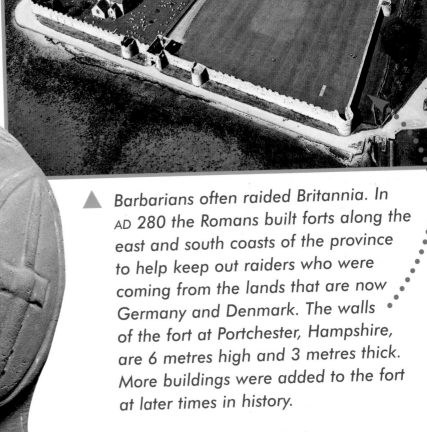

▲ Barbarians often raided Britannia. In AD 280 the Romans built forts along the east and south coasts of the province to help keep out raiders who were coming from the lands that are now Germany and Denmark. The walls of the fort at Portchester, Hampshire, are 6 metres high and 3 metres thick. More buildings were added to the fort at later times in history.

◀ A Roman figure of a Barbarian.

After the Romans

The Roman army left Britannia but other Romans stayed, working their farms and running businesses in towns. For some time life carried on as if Britain was still a Roman province. Some towns continued to be run in Roman ways, possibly for hundreds of years.

Less trade and smaller towns

Most Roman coins were made to pay soldiers' wages. After the legions left, no more Roman money reached Britain. Without money, trade and industry declined. Craftsmen could no longer earn a living and went back to farming or moved abroad to provide for their families.

The Roman army had looked after the roads and kept them well repaired. Without the soldiers, the roads were not mended and became more difficult to travel along. This also led to a decline in trade.

With less trade taking place, towns became smaller. There were fewer skilled craftsmen and so many buildings could not be repaired. Some people went back to living in hill forts.

▼ *Roman buildings decayed as they were no longer used or looked after. Stones were taken for new buildings. This was the Roman theatre at St Albans. Remains like these are cared for now, as part of Britain's history.*

Life in the countryside

Life in the countryside continued much as before. It had never been heavily affected by Roman rule, so its removal made little difference. Most Britons were still farmers. They had continued mostly to barter their goods and so the disappearance of coins did not affect them much. Wealthy farmers stayed running their Roman-style villas, although over time these began to look less Roman.

A new invasion

The people who raided Britain from Germany and Denmark became known as Anglo-Saxons. In AD 449 a British leader asked some Anglo-Saxons to help him fight off other raiders in the north. The Anglo-Saxons helped, but then decided to settle in Britain themselves. In some places they fought the Britons, but in others they lived peacefully with them. Over time it became difficult to tell them apart.

Roman remains

The Romans had little effect on the lives of many Britons, but the roads and towns they built had a lasting effect on the British landscape. You may be able to visit the remains of a Roman town, fort, villa, theatre or amphitheatre and see Roman artefacts on display at a museum.

Look back through the pictures in this book. Which type of Roman site would you most like to visit? Think of three things that you would like to find out there.

▲ *In a display of Roman artefacts you might see a strigil. Find out how this was used at the Roman baths.*

▶ *A pair of tweezers and a manicure set. What do these objects tell you about people in Roman Britain?*

Glossary

AD
stands for 'Anno Domini', the Latin for 'in the year of the Lord'. This refers to Jesus, whom Christians call 'Lord'. The time when Jesus was born was taken as the year 0. Dates after this are called AD, and dates before are called BC.

allies
people or countries who have agreed to help one another.

amphitheatre
an oval area surrounded by seating, where gladiator games and wild animal shows were performed.

amphorae
two-handled jars for holding liquid.

archaeologists
people who find out about the past by looking at the remains that people have left behind.

artefacts
man-made objects, e.g. pottery or tools.

ballista bolt
an arrow-like object fired from a two-man weapon, like a large crossbow.

barrack
a building to house soldiers.

barter
to trade by exchanging goods, after agreeing they are of the same value.

basilica
a large building serving as the centre of government of a Roman town.

BC
stands for 'Before Christ'. 'Christ' is a name that Christians give to Jesus. In dates, a number followed by BC means that number of years before the time when Jesus was born.

Britons
inhabitants of Britain at the time the Romans invaded. Today they are often called 'Celts', but neither they nor the Romans used this term.

cavalry
soldiers on horseback, making up part of an army.

Celts
a word used today to describe many tribes in Europe who lived alongside or were conquered by the Romans.

chieftain
the leader of a tribe or group.

citizen
in the Roman Empire, a free person with the right to vote.

city-state
a city from which a region of land was controlled.

civilised
well-behaved, according to the rules and expectations of a developed society.

civil war
a war between two or more armies from the same country or Empire.

clerk
someone whose work required reading, writing and arithmetic skills.

conquer
to gain control of something, by force.

councillors
Roman citizens responsible for running a town, with duties such as supervising tax collection and making laws.

decline
to slowly get worse.

emigrate
to leave a country to settle in another.

Empire
an area of land ruled by an emperor or government.

evidence
a piece of information which can be taken to help prove an idea.

excavation
careful digging up of an area of land in search of information about the past.

export
to sell goods produced in one country to another.

fort
a strongly defended place.

forum	a large open area in the centre of a Roman town, used as a meeting and market place.
general	a leader in the army.
gladiator	a man who took part in dangerous fights put on as entertainment.
governor	a Roman appointed by the Emperor to rule a province. The governor collected taxes, enforced laws and controlled the army in the province.
granary	a building designed to store food, usually grain.
heirs	people who will take over a person's position or wealth when he or she dies.
hill fort	an area, usually on top of a hill, surrounded by banks and ditches for defence.
import	to buy goods from another country.
inscription	writing carved on something.
invade	to enter a country with the intention of conquering it.
legion	a unit of Roman soldiers, numbering 3,000 to 5,000 men.
legionary	a Roman foot soldier.
maritime	near the sea.
massacred	violently killed.
military	to do with war.
mosaic	a pattern made with small coloured stone cubes, called tesserae.
municipium	a town with special status in the Roman Empire.
neutral	not supporting either side in an argument or a war.
province	a division of the Roman Empire.
raids	rapid, surprise attacks on a country.
rampart	a raised bank of earth, usually for defence, often with a wooden fence on top and a ditch around the outside.
reconstruction	a drawing or model of what something may have been like, based on evidence.
revolt	to rise up against a ruler.
scribe	someone whose job was to write things down. Not everyone could read and write in the Roman world, so scribes did this for them.
settle	to set up a permanent home.
settlement	the permanent home of a community.
shrine	a special place associated with a god or goddess.
stonemason	a builder in stone.
temperate	neither very hot nor very cold.
temple	a building for religious worship.
tesserae	the small pieces making up a mosaic.
toga	a garment worn by a Roman citizen. It was a long cloth wound round the body and draped over the shoulder.
torc	a piece of jewellery made of twisted metal, worn around the neck or arm.
tribe	a group of people living in an area, who shared a common way of life.
villa	a Roman agricultural complex. 'Villa' could mean the main farmhouse or the whole estate of buildings and fields.
warrior class	the top level of society in pre-Roman Britain. Warriors specialised in feasting and fighting.

For teachers and parents

For over 350 years the Roman Empire brought together a huge expanse of territories. Before the Romans arrived in Britain, the Britons had their own culture. Some did not like the newcomers. Others welcomed them. The Roman conquest of the country began with the Claudian invasion in AD 43 but was not secure until after the Boudican revolt of AD 60-61. Tribes from eastern England led by Queen Boudica destroyed three major Roman towns and may have been on the brink of victory before their final defeat.

Often 'Celt' is used as a convenient shorthand term for the pre-Roman inhabitants of Britain. This is misleading. The people identified themselves by their tribal name, although the different tribes shared a similar culture. Contemporary writers did not use the term 'Celt' when referring to the people of Britain. 'Britons' has been used in this book.

After the conquest the Romans built many formally laid-out towns. Native British farms continued in some parts of the countryside while villa estates developed in others. Some of these would have been owned by Britons, others by newcomers.

At the end of the Roman period the legions were removed and towns decayed. People returned to farming, a system that would have been familiar to the Britons 350 years previously. New tribes such as the Angles, Saxons and Scots raided and finally came to settle here.

Our knowledge of events and life in Roman Britain comes from archaeology, inscriptions and written documents. There is a wide range of sites and museums for children to explore. Studying this period therefore provides an opportunity to develop children's historical skills particularly in understanding the range and nature of the evidence available and in making inferences from it. In addition, the activities suggested in this book provide opportunities for cross-curricular work relating to literacy, mathematics and design, technology and ICT.

SUGGESTED FURTHER ACTIVITIES

Pages 4 – 5 Timeline
As well as a class timeline, you could make a display with a world map, showing countries from which people have moved to Britain. Investigate the routes and transport they would have used, and the parts of Britain where they would have arrived.

Pages 6 – 7 Find out about the Britons
Let the children think about the differences between documentary and archaeological evidence, for learning about the past. Can written sources be trusted? Does archaeology tell us all we need to know?

Does Julius Caesar tell us much about the Britons' lifestyle, or only about parts of it? What aspects does he not discuss? Has he any

reasons to lie? (E.g. he says that Britons are warriors, whereas archaeological evidence suggests they were farmers.) A translation of Book 5 of The Gallic Wars by Julius Caesar, including his descriptions of the Britons, is at: http://classics.mit.edu/Caesar/gallic.5.5.html.

For thinking about archaeological sources, you could bring in a range of objects that might be thrown away. Help the children decide which of these objects would survive to be dug up in the future and which would rot away. Would all or only part of the object survive? Groups of children could pick one room of a house and decide which objects in it would survive for 2,000 years. Then they should draw these objects and see if other groups can identify the room.

Pages 8 – 9 How were the Romans different?
Useful websites for further research are:
http://www.roman-empire.net/maps/map-empire.html (an interactive map of the Roman Empire);
http://www.bbc.co.uk/schools/primaryhistory/romans/;
http://library.thinkquest.org/22866/English/Leger.html#soldaat (The life of a Roman Soldier).

For the table of differences between Romans and Britons, children could identify categories (e.g. work, buildings, clothing) for the first column, and fill in details in 'Romans' and 'Britons' columns.

Pages 10 – 11 The Romans invade Britain
Let the children try to rank these reasons why the Romans invaded Britain. Then discuss, encouraging them to give reasons for their order.

- Emperor Claudius was not popular. A victory might change this.
- Britain was thought to be wealthy, full of silver and wheat.
- Some British kings had asked the Romans to help protect their kingdoms from rivals.
- Troublemakers in Gaul could escape from the Romans to Britain.
- Some British tribes were trading with the Romans.
- Some British tribes were raiding Gaul and damaging Roman property.
- More slaves were always needed to provide labour in the Empire.

Pages 12 – 13 The start of a revolt
Let the children look at interpretations of Boudica over time (Cassius Dio's account, Victorian sculpture and paintings, modern films). How has her appearance changed? How has it stayed the same? Why might this be? Is any representation likely to be the most accurate?

Pages 14 – 15 Boudica's revolt

The Romans were vastly outnumbered in the final battle with Boudica, but were better trained. They also used different weapons and methods of defence from the Britons. Children could research these and consider which aspects may have given the Romans an advantage in hand-to-hand fighting.

Pages 16 – 17 The effects of the revolt

A plan of Housesteads fort can be found at: http://www.roman-britain.org/places/images/vercovicium_plan.gif. Children could also look at: http://vindolanda.csad.ox.ac.uk/exhibition/army-1.shtml. Let the children compare fort plans and see how the layout stays the same. Discuss the advantages (familiarity, and soldiers could be posted regularly to different forts).

Most forts had a 'vicus' attached to them – a shanty town of goods and services that supplied the troops.

Pages 18 – 19 The province of Britannia

Children could find out about the layout of Roman towns from: http://www.roman-britain.org/rb_towns.htm.

They could design a mosaic floor of their own. Many British mosaics had patterns or flower designs, but some showed gods and people.

Pages 20 – 21 How the Romans changed Britain

Information about some of the main Roman roads in Britain can be found at http://www.channel4.com/history/microsites/T/timeteam/snapshot_romanroads.html.

Some role-play would help children to understand bartering.

Foods introduced to Britain by the Romans include: white carrots, liquamen (fish sauce; Worcester sauce is thought to be somewhat similar), dates, olives (and olive oil), radishes, garlic, onions, walnuts, leeks, figs, chestnuts, almonds, lettuce, parsnips, broad beans, cabbages, plums, damsons, cherries, apples.
Foods already in Britain include: milk, soft cheese, bread, bacon, beef, oysters, lamb, pig, hazelnuts, nettles, dandelions, Celtic beans (a smaller version of the broad bean), raspberries, blackberries, elderberries, strawberries, crab apples, honey, hare, geese.
You might allow the children to prepare and try a selection of 'typical' Roman foods.

Look at pictures of Roman coins, for example, at http://www.romancoins.info/Content.html. Who was important enough to appear on the coins? (The Emperor, the army, gods.) What messages did the coins convey? (E.g. propaganda such as 'The Emperor is strong and just'; 'The Empire is being well cared for'.)

Pages 22 – 23 How did Britain stay the same?

Let the children practise using Roman numerals.
I = 1; V = 5; X = 10; L = 50; C = 100; D = 500; M = 1,000.
A smaller number before a larger one subtracts from it. E.g.: IX = 9.
A smaller number after a larger one adds to it. E.g.: XXXII = 32.

Bring in suitable cloth for the children to dress up in a toga over their own clothes. Discuss why such clothing, on its own, might be impractical. Why would trousers, tunics and cloaks, worn by the Britons, be better?

Pages 24 – 25 The end of Roman Britain

The children could do some further research on the Barbarians at: http://rome.mrdonn.org/barbarians.html.

Pages 26 – 27 After the Romans

Let the children think about how people might pay for things without money. Is this harder or easier than using money? Do we always use money today when we buy things?

How different was Britain after the Romans left, compared with before they arrived? In a class discussion, let the children put forward ideas for lists of what had changed and what had stayed the same.

PLACES TO VISIT

Cardiff: National Museums & Galleries of Wales (www.museumwales.ac.uk)
Chester: Grosvenor Museum (www.grosvenormuseum.co.uk)
Chichester: Fishbourne Roman Palace (www.fishbourneromanpalace.com)
Cirencester: Corinium Museum (www.cotswold.gov.uk)
Colchester: Castle Museum (www.colchestermuseums.org.uk)
Edinburgh: Museum of Scotland (www.nms.ac.uk)
Leicester: Jewry Wall Museum (www.leicester.gov.uk/museums)
London: British Museum (www.britishmuseum.org)
        Museum of London (www.museumoflondon.org.uk)
Newcastle: Great North Museum (www.twmuseums.org.uk)
Reading: Museum of Reading (www.readingmuseum.org.uk)
St Albans: Verulamium Museum (www.stalbansmuseums.org.uk)
York: Yorkshire Museum & Gardens (www.yorkshiremuseum.org.uk)

Arbeia Roman Fort, South Shields (www.twmuseums.org.uk)
Housesteads Roman Fort, Hexham (www.english-heritage.org.uk)
Lunt Roman Fort, Baginton (www.luntromanfort.org.uk)
Segedunum Roman Fort, Wallsend (www.twmuseums.org.uk)

Chedworth Roman Villa, Yanworth, Cheltenham (www.ntrust.org.uk)
Lullingstone Roman Villa, Eynsford (www.english-heritage.org.uk)

Caerwent Roman Town (off the A48 between Caerleon & Chepstow)
Wroxeter Roman Town (www.english-heritage.org.uk)

Bath Roman Baths (www.romanbaths.co.uk)
Segedunum Bath House, Wallsend (www.twmuseums.org.uk)

Verulamium Theatre, St Albans (www.romantheatre.co.uk)

Caerleon Amphitheatre (off Lodge Rd, Caerleon)
Silchester Amphitheatre (off Wall Lane, Nr Silchester)

Dolacauthi gold mines

Index